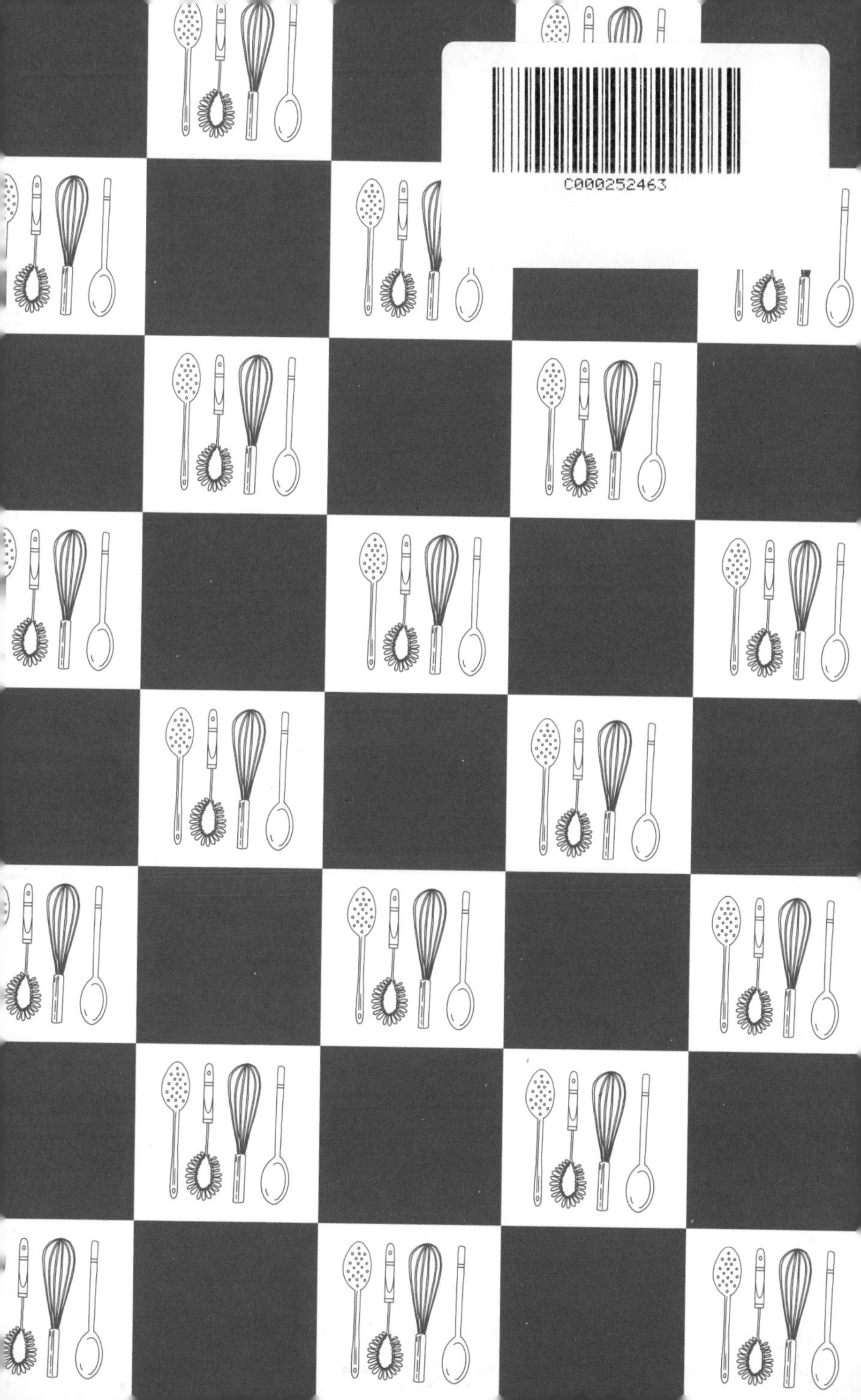

CLASSIC COCKTAILS

Editor:
Valerie Ferguson

LORENZ BOOKS

Contents

Introduction

The cocktail, a drink taken as an appetizer before a meal, was traditionally made from only two spirits or liqueurs, but today it may also include such exotic ingredients as coconut milk and tropical fruits. While simple classic cocktails, like the Margarita and Mint Julep, have not lost their popularity, they have been joined by more elaborate mixtures, such as Blue Hawaiian and Mai Tai.

Learn how to make these and many more with the help of this book, which gives clear instructions for all kinds of classic and sophisticated cocktails, through the short and lively, to the long, cooling and thirst-quenching – not forgetting delicious non-alcoholic creations. There is also plenty of practical information on ingredients, equipment and techniques.

You will see how easy it is to produce all kinds of glorious cocktails at home with no more than a cocktail shaker, large glass jug, blender and a few essential ingredients such as bitters, sugar syrup, ice and, of course, a couple of bottles of your favourite spirits and liqueurs. Most of the drinks are quick and easy to make, so next time you plan to entertain add to the fun of the occasion by serving a choice of cocktails.

Ingredients & Garnishes

Cocktails are made from a wide variety of easily obtained ingredients, but do not forget to include the garnishes when you shop.

Spirits

Brandy is distilled from grape wines and is also available in fruit flavours such as apricot and apple (Calvados). Gin, a colourless spirit distilled from grains and flavourings, combines successfully with many fruit juices, vermouth and liqueurs to create some of the classic cocktails. Rum, distilled from sugar cane and molasses, is available dark or white and with flavourings; it is popular for flamboyant cocktails such as Planter's Punch. Mexican Tequila is fermented and distilled from agave cactus juice; it is the essential ingredient of a Margarita cocktail. Vodka, colourless and with a neutral taste, mixes well with other pirits and fruit juices such as orange or grapefuit. Whisky is available in several types: Scotch whisky, Irish whiskey, American bourbon and Canadian rye.

Wines

Use *brut* (dry) champagne or sparkling wines when making cocktails. Ginger wine, sweet, golden and aromatic, combines well with spirits and red wine. Sherry is a fortified wine, originally from Spain, available as pale and dry, medium dry, medium and sweet. Vermouth is a high-strength wine blended with herbs. It may be extra-dry white, bitter-sweet rosé, medium-sweet bianco or sweet red.

Cider

Made from fermented apple juice, sweet or dry cider mixes well with brandy and other spirits.

Liqueurs

Amaretto has a sweet almond and apricot flavour, and is used in cocktails such as Hooded Claw. Anisettes, or aniseed-flavoured liqueurs, include Sambucca, Pernod and pastis. Benedictine and Chartreuse are brandy-based and flavoured with honey, herbs and spices. Cointreau, triple sec, curaçao and Grand Marnier are orange-flavoured. Cream liqueurs, such as Bailey's Irish Cream, contain cream and other flavourings. Crème de cacao has a cocoa-vanilla taste, and

Left: Cocktails are served in glasses of all shapes and sizes.

Above: A spring of fresh mint adds colour as well as a fresh, sweet taste.

crème de cassis is a blackcurrant liqueur. Sweet, peppermint-flavoured crème de menthe also includes spices. Golden-coloured Galliano is flavoured with licorice and aniseed. Kahlúa and Tia Maria are coffee-based. Southern Comfort has a bourbon base flavoured with fruit.

Mixers & Juices

Lemon, ginger ale, lemonade, cola, soda water and tonic water are good for providing length to a cocktail. A wide range of fruit juices may also be used, including apple, cranberry, orange, pineapple, pink grapefruit, prune, red grape and tomato. Coconut milk and cream, however, are mainly used in tropical cocktails. Passion-fruit cordial and nectar, made with concentrated juice and natural flavourings, are used in exotic cocktails.

Right: Green olives are often used as a finishing touch in cocktails.

Added Flavours

The little extras that give zing to a cocktail include the widely used angostura bitters, grenadine syrup and Worcestershire and Tabasco sauces. Fresh mint, lemon balm, grated nutmeg, cinnamon sticks and a pinch of cayenne can all be used to pep up basic punches.

Garnishes

Citrus fruit, particularly lemons, are widely used. An extensive range of other fruits find a place in exotic cocktails, including strawberries, pineapples and prickly pears. The popular maraschino cherry is a cherry that has been preserved in maraschino liqueur; it gives the final touch to cocktails such as Blue Hawaiian. Some Martinis require a green olive, while the Gibson calls for a pearl onion. Grated chocolate and nutmeg adorn egg-nogs and flips. Decorations such as paper umbrellas, fireworks and twisted, coloured straws add a final touch of fun to a cocktail.

Glasses

Whatever the cocktail, it is important to choose the right glass.

Cocktail or Martini Glass

With a wide conical bowl on a tall stem, this holds about 150 ml/¼ pint/⅔ cup.

Collins Glass

The tallest of the tumblers, narrow with perfectly straight sides, this holds about 300 ml/½ pint/ 1¼ cups and is typically used for long drinks.

Shorts Tumbler

This is used for shorter drinks, which are served "on the rocks". It holds about 175 ml/6 fl oz/¾ cup.

Highball Glass

This is a medium-sized tumbler (*see above*) and is the glass most used. It holds about 250 ml/8 fl oz/1 cup.

Liqueur Glass

A tiny glass for small measures about 50 ml/2 fl oz/¼ cup.

Brandy Balloon or Snifter

This glass has been designed to trap the distinctive fragrance of the brandy in the bowl of the glass.

Sherry Glass

Varying in size and shape, this is used for serving shorter cocktails including port-based cocktails.

Champagne Glass

This is the more traditional shape: the tall, slim flute. It is more efficient at conserving the fizz.

Red Wine Balloon

The most useful size of wine glass, holding 300 ml/½ pint/ 1¼ cups. It is normally filled to only half-capacity to allow the wine to be swirled around inside.

White Wine Glass

A long-stemmed medium-size glass that keeps warm hands away from the chilled wine or cocktail.

Champagne Glass (bowl)

The alternative shaped glass for champagne. It is traditionally used where additional decorations (such as pieces of fruit) are added to the rim.

Equipment

A few essential pieces of equipment are needed to make successful cocktails.

Opening & Measuring

• **Corkscrew** The fold-away type, with a can opener and bottle-top opener, is the most useful.

• **Tot measures or measuring jug** For measuring out the required quantities. The measurements can be in single (25 ml/1½ tbsp) or double (45 ml/3 tbsp) bar measures, fluid ounces or millilitres.

Preparation

• **Lemon knife and squeezer** A good-quality sharp knife is required for cutting fruit and the squeezer for extracting juice.

• **Muddler** A long stick with a bulbous end, which is used for crushing sugar or mint leaves. A pestle and mortar can be used instead.

• **Sieve** (strainer) Sometimes used for preparing fresh-fruit cocktails.

• **Whisk** For beating egg in flips.

• **Zester and cannelle knife** For presenting fruit when dressing glasses.

Blending & Pouring

• **Bar spoon** A long-handled spoon used for mixing the drink directly in the glass.

• **Cocktail shaker** Used for those cocktails made with juice and syrups that need good mixing but do not depend upon being crystal clear.

• **Goblet blender** For mixing cocktails that need to be aerated, to create a frothy cocktail.

Above: Items for the well-stocked bar.

• **Mixing jug or bar glass** For drinks that are not shaken and are meant to be clear. It should be large enough to hold two or three drinks.

• **Strainer** Used when pouring drinks from shaker or bar glass to cocktail glass.

Ice Preparation

• **Ice bag or cloth** Essential for holding ice cubes when crushing, either to roughly cracked lumps or to fine snow.

• **Wooden mallet** For crushing the ice; the end of a wooden rolling pin will also work well.

Garnishing

• **Nutmeg grater** Used for grating the nut over egg-nogs and frothy drinks.

• **Straw, swizzle sticks and cocktail sticks** Used for the finishing decorative touches that complete a cocktail.

Techniques

Cocktails are simple to prepare and only require a few basic skills.

Crushing Ice

Cracked and crushed ice and ice snow are easily made, but do not be tempted to crush ice in a blender or food processor as it will blunt the blade.

1 Lay a clean dishtowel on a work surface and cover half with ice cubes. Fold the towel over. Alternatively, place the ice cubes in a cloth ice bag.

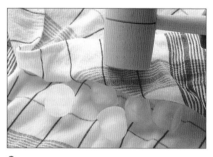

2 Using the end of a rolling pin or a wooden mallet, strike the ice firmly several times, until you achieve the required fineness. Store cracked or crushed ice in the freezer in small plastic bags; use fine ice snow immediately it is made.

Making Decorative Ice Cubes

Decorative ice cubes can instantly jazz up simple cocktails. Flavour and colour ice cubes with fruit juices or bitters and freeze as normal.

1 Fill each compartment of an ice-cube tray half-full with water and place in the freezer for 2–3 hours, or until the water has frozen.

2 Prepare the fruit, olives, mint leaves, lemon rind, raisins or borage flowers and dip each briefly in water. Place in the ice-cube trays and freeze again. Top up the trays with water and return to the freezer to freeze completely.

Frosting Glasses

A sugar or salt frosting adds to both the look and taste of a cocktail. Celery salt, grated coconut or chocolate, coloured sugars or cocoa can also be used for a similar effect. Place the frosted glass in the fridge to chill until you are ready to serve the cocktail.

1 Hold the glass upside-down, so that the juice does not run down the glass. Rub the rim of the glass with the cut surface of a lemon, lime, orange or even a slice of fresh pineapple.

2 Keeping the glass upside-down and holding the base, dip the rim into a shallow layer of sugar or salt. Re-dip the glass, if necessary, so that the rim is well-coated. Stand the glass upright and leave until the frosting has dried, then chill.

Shaking & Stirring Cocktails

As a general rule, the simpler cocktails and those that are served clear are just stirred over ice, in a glass, before being strained into a serving glass. Cocktails that contain sugar syrups or creams require more than just a stir and are combined and chilled by briefly shaking together with ice. Remember that it is only possible to shake one or two servings at a time.

1 To shake a cocktail, fill the cocktail shaker two-thirds full with ice cubes and pour in the spirits; add the mixers, if not sparkling, and the flavouring ingredients. Put on the lid and hold firmly in place with one hand while holding the shaker in the other hand.

2 Shake the cocktail vigorously for about 10 seconds to blend simple concoctions and for 20–30 seconds for drinks with sugar syrups or eggs. By this time the outside of the shaker should feel chilled.

3 Remove the small lid and pour into the prepared glass, using a strainer if the shaker is not already fitted with one to remove any particles.

Basic Recipes

Use these recipes to create some of the exciting cocktails in this book.

Sugar Syrup

A sugar syrup is sometimes preferable to crystal sugars for sweetening cocktails, since it immediately blends with the other ingredients.

Makes about 750 ml/1¼ pints/ 3 cups

INGREDIENTS
350 g/12 oz/1¾ cups caster (superfine) sugar
600 ml/20fl oz/2½ cups water

1 Heat the sugar and water gently in a heavy pan, stirring until the sugar has dissolved. Brush the sides of the pan with a dampened pastry brush to remove any sugar crystals.

2 Bring to the boil and boil for 3–5 minutes. Skim off any scum and remove the pan from the heat. Cool. Store in sterilized, airtight bottles in the fridge for up to 1 month.

Flavoured Syrups

Syrup can be flavoured with any ingredient you like. Add to the basic sugar syrup, bring to the boil, then bottle and store.

Makes about 450 ml/¾ pint/ scant 2 cups

INGREDIENTS
900 g/2 lb very ripe soft or stone fruit, such as raspberries, black or redcurrants, plums or peaches, washed
350 g/12 oz/1¾ cups caster (superfine) sugar

1 Place the fruit in a bowl and crush using the end of a rolling pin, a wooden pestle or a potato masher. Cover and leave overnight.

2 Strain the purée through muslin (cheesecloth). Twist the corners of the cloth together tightly. Measure the juice and add 225 g/8 oz/1 cup sugar to every 300 ml/10fl oz/1¼ cups. Heat gently, stirring, until the sugar has dissolved. Continue as for sugar syrup.

Flavoured Spirits

Gin, vodka and white rum can be left to infuse and absorb the flavours of a wide variety of soft fruits.

Makes 1.2 litres/2 pints/5 cups

INGREDIENTS
450 g/1 lb raspberries, strawberries, pineapple or sloes
225 g/ 8 oz/generous 1 cup caster (superfine) sugar
1 litre/1¾ pints/4 cups gin or vodka

1 Place the fruit in a wide-necked jar and add the sugar. If using sloes, prick them with a fine skewer to release their flavour. Add the spirit. Cover tightly. Leave in a cool, dark place for a month, shaking gently every week.

2 Strain through muslin (cheesecloth) and squeeze out the rest of the liquid from the fruit. Pour the flavoured spirit into a sterilized bottle, seal and store in a cool, dark place.

COOK'S TIP: To sterilize bottles soak them for 5 minutes in boiling water, then dry in a medium oven.

Steeped Spirits

Strongly tasting ingredients, such as chillies, can be steeped in any spirit to create an interesting flavour.

Makes 1 litre/1¾ pints/4 cups

INGREDIENTS
25–50 g/1–2 oz small red chillies, or to taste
1 litre/1¾ pints/4 cups sherry or vodka

1 Wash and dry the red chillies, discarding any that are less than perfect. Using a cocktail stick, prick the chillies all over so that their flavour will be released.

2 Pack the chillies tightly into a sterilized bottle. Top up with sherry or vodka. Fit the cork tightly and leave in a dark place for at least 10 days or up to 2 months before using.

Kir Lethale

The raisins for this cocktail should be soaked overnight in vodka.

Serves 6

INGREDIENTS
6 vodka-soaked raisins
30 ml/2 tbsp vodka or raisin vodka
3 measures/70 ml/4½ tbsp crème de cassis
1 bottle *brut* champagne or
 dry sparkling wine, chilled

1 Place a vodka-soaked raisin at the bottom of each wine glass.

2 Add 5ml/1 tsp vodka or the vodka from the steeped raisins, if you like, to each glass.

3 Divide the crème de cassis equally among the glasses.

4 When you are ready to serve, top up each glass with the champagne or dry sparkling wine.

Apricot Bellini

This is a version of the famous apéritif served at Harry's Bar in Venice.

Serves 6–8

INGREDIENTS
3 apricots
10 ml/2 tsp lemon juice
10 ml/2 tsp sugar syrup
   (see Basic Recipes page 12)
2 measures/45 ml/3 tbsp apricot brandy
   or peach schnapps
1 bottle *brut* champagne or
   dry sparkling wine, chilled

1 Plunge the apricots into boiling
water for 2 minutes to loosen the
skins. Peel off the skins, remove the
stones and discard both.

2 Process the apricot flesh with the
lemon juice in a food processor until
you have a smooth purée. Sweeten to
taste with sugar syrup, then sieve.

3 Add the brandy or peach schnapps
to the apricot nectar and mix together.
Divide the mixture among chilled
champagne flutes. Top up with chilled
champagne or sparkling wine and serve.

VARIATION: Instead of apricots
and apricot brandy, use fresh
raspberries and raspberry-infused
gin or syrup.

Tequila Sunrise

The red grenadine in this drink glows in the glass like the sun rising.

Serves 1

INGREDIENTS
60 ml/4 tbsp freshly squeezed orange juice
juice of 1 lime
crushed ice
1 measure/25 ml/1½ tbsp golden tequila
5 ml/1 tsp grenadine

1 Squeeze the orange and lime juices just before making the cocktail. Do not use orange juice from a carton or bottled lime juice, or the flavour of the finished drink will be spoiled.

2 Half-fill a cocktail glass with crushed ice. Pour in the tequila, followed by the orange and lime juices.

3 Quickly add the grenadine, pouring it over the back of a teaspoon held in the glass so that it sinks to the bottom of the drink. Serve immediately.

VARIATION: To make a Pink Cadillac, use Grand Marnier instead of orange juice.

Margarita

This renowned tequila cocktail can be served using ice in one of two ways.

Serves 1

INGREDIENTS

45 ml/3 tbsp tequila
1 measure/25 ml/1½ tbsp curaçao triple sec
1 measure/25 ml/1½ tbsp freshly squeezed
    lime juice
lime wedge and salt, for frosting the glass
crushed ice or ice cubes, to serve

1 Frost a cocktail glass by rubbing the outer rim with the wedge of lime. It is important that there is no salt inside the glass, so take care that lime juice is applied only to the outer rim. Dip the glass in a saucer of salt so that the rim is evenly coated. Allow to dry.

2 Combine the tequila, triple sec and lime juice in a cocktail shaker, add crushed ice, if using, and shake to mix.

3 Carefully pour into the frosted glass. If crushed ice is not used, place ice cubes in the glass and then pour the mixture over the top.

Frozen Strawberry Daiquiri

A version of the Cuban original, which was made only with local Cuban rum, lime juice, ice and sugar.

Serves 1

INGREDIENTS
ice cubes
4 whole strawberries
10 ml/2 tsp lime juice
1 measure/25 ml/1½ tbsp brandy
 or strawberry brandy
1 measure/25 ml/1½ tbsp
 white rum
dash of grenadine
strawberry and a sprig of fresh mint,
 to decorate

3 Add the white rum, grenadine and half a glass of finely crushed ice to the blender and process once more, to a smooth slush. Pour the mixture into a well-chilled cocktail glass.

1 Place several ice cubes in a clean, folded dishtowel and crush to a fine snow, using a rolling pin or hammer.

2 Place the strawberries with the lime juice and brandy in a blender and process to a purée.

4 To decorate, remove the hull from the strawberry and replace with a small sprig of fresh mint.

VARIATION: Substitute 50 ml/ 2 fl oz/¼ cup cream for the rum and brandy. Process in the blender and serve as a non-alcoholic daiquiri.

5 Make a cut in the side of the strawberry and attach to the rim of the glass. Serve immediately with a short straw, if you like.

COOK'S TIP: When strawberries are out of season, use drained, canned ones instead.

Mint Julep

One of the oldest cocktails, this originated in the southern states of America. Add fresh mint leaves according to taste.

Serves 1

INGREDIENTS
15 ml/1 tbsp caster (superfine) sugar
8–10 fresh mint leaves
15 ml/1 tbsp hot water
crushed ice
2 measures/45 ml/3 tbsp bourbon or whisky

3 Spoon into a snifter or brandy balloon and half-fill with crushed ice. Add the bourbon or whisky.

1 Place the sugar in a pestle and mortar or in a bar glass with a muddler. Tear the mint leaves into small pieces and add to the sugar.

4 Stir until the outside of the glass has frosted. Allow to stand for a couple of minutes, to let the ice melt slightly and dilute the drink. Serve with straws, if liked.

VARIATION: Add some chilled soda water to the julep for a refreshing, long drink.

2 Bruise the mint leaves to release their flavour and colour. Add the hot water and grind well together.

Bloody Maria

This simple cocktail has a spicy flavour from the addition of Tabasco.

Serves 1

INGREDIENTS
5 measures/120 ml/4 fl oz/½ cup tomato
  juice, chilled
30 ml/2 tbsp tequila
2.5 ml/½ tsp Worcestershire sauce
few drops of Tabasco sauce
10 ml/2 tsp lemon
pinch of celery salt
salt and ground black pepper
ice cubes and 1 celery stick, cut into
  batons, to serve

1 Mix the tomato juice, tequila and Worcestershire sauce in a jug.

2 Stir the mixture well. Add a few drops of Tabasco sauce and the lemon juice and stir again.

3 Taste and season with celery salt, salt and pepper. Serve in shorts glasses over ice cubes, with celery batons.

Golden Start

A delicious mix of Galliano, orange, pineapple and coconut cream.

Serves 1

INGREDIENTS
2 measures/45 ml/3 tbsp Galliano
1 measure/25 ml/1½ tbsp orange
    juice, chilled
1 measure/25 ml/1½ tbsp pineapple
    juice, chilled
1 measure/25 ml/1½ tbsp white or
    orange curaçao
1 measure/25 ml/1½ tbsp coconut cream
15 ml/1 tbsp fine ice snow
30 ml/2 tbsp pineapple juice and caster
    (superfine) sugar, to frost the glass

1 Put the Galliano, orange and pineapple juices and curaçao in a blender and process together.

2 Add the coconut cream with the fine ice snow and process until frothy.

3 Rub the rim of a cocktail glass or shorts tumbler with pineapple juice and invert the glass into a saucer of sugar, to frost the rim. Pour the cocktail into the prepared glass while still frothy and serve at once.

23

Singapore Sling

The origins of this old-fashioned thirst-quencher lie in South-east Asia. The drink is served without mixing so that the cherry brandy rises up from the base of the cocktail.

Serves 1

INGREDIENTS
2 measures/45 ml/3 tbsp gin
cracked ice
juice of 1 lemon
5 ml/1 tsp caster (superfine) sugar
soda water, chilled
15 ml/1 tbsp Cointreau
15 ml/1 tbsp cherry brandy
1 lemon and 1 black cherry, to decorate

3 To decorate, use a vegetable peeler or sharp knife to cut a long, thin piece of rind round and round the lemon.

1 Pour the gin into a tall glass of ice and mix with the lemon juice and sugar. Strain the cocktail into a highball glass full of cracked ice.

2 Top up the cocktail with chilled soda water, to taste. Add the Cointreau and the cherry brandy, but do not stir.

4 Arrange the strip of lemon rind in the glass. Thread the black cherry on to two cocktail sticks and add to the rim of the glass. Add a swizzle stick. Serve the cocktail immediately.

VARIATIONS: Substitute Benedictine for the Cointreau for a Straits Sling, or add ginger beer instead of soda water for a Raffles Bar Sling.

Harvey Wallbanger

Orange juice and vodka are given a lift with a dash of Galliano. Those who like a stronger version could add an extra measure of vodka.

Serves 1

INGREDIENTS
1 measure/25 ml/1½ tbsp vodka
15 ml/1 tbsp Galliano
7 measures/160 ml/5 fl oz/⅔ cup
   orange juice
cracked ice and ice cubes
1 small orange, to decorate

1 Pour the vodka, Galliano and orange juice into a tall glass of ice. Mix the cocktail and ice for about 30 seconds, to chill it well.

VARIATIONS: For a Screwdriver, omit the Galliano. For Buck's Fizz, another classic cocktail based on orange juice, pour 5 measures/ 120 ml/4 fl oz/½ cup fresh orange juice and 5 ml/1 tsp grenadine into a chilled glass. Add 200 ml/7 fl oz/ scant 1 cup chilled champagne. Omit the fruit slices and serve in a champagne flute.

2 Using a cannelle knife (zester), take a series of thin strips of rind off the orange, running from the top to the bottom of the fruit.

3 Using a small, sharp knife, thinly slice half the orange horizontally.

4 Cut the orange slices in half and wedge 3 or 4 slices between cracked ice in a highball glass. Use the other orange half in another cocktail.

5 Strain the chilled cocktail into the prepared glass and serve at once.

Kew Pimm's

A very drinkable concoction of sweet vermouth, curaçao, vodka, gin and cherry brandy served over summer fruit.

Serves 1

INGREDIENTS
1 measure/25 ml/1½ tbsp sweet vermouth
1 measure/25 ml/1½ tbsp orange curaçao
15 ml/1 tbsp vodka
15 ml/1 tbsp gin
15 ml/1 tbsp cherry brandy
ice cubes
assorted soft summer fruits, such as
    strawberries, raspberries and redcurrants
1–2 dashes angostura bitters
2 measures/45 ml/3 tbsp American dry
    ginger ale, chilled
2 measures/45 ml/3 tbsp
    lemonade, chilled
1 lemon and fresh lemon balm or mint
    leaves, to decorate

1 Measure the vermouth, curaçao, vodka, gin and cherry brandy into a large glass of ice and stir well to chill.

2 Place ice cubes and soft summer fruits in a Collins glass. Strain the cocktail into the glass.

3 Add the bitters and then pour in equal quantities of chilled ginger ale and lemonade to taste.

4 To make a decorative lemon triangle, pare a thin piece of rind from the lemon. Cut the rind into a rectangle and cut a slit three-quarters of the way across it. Turn the rectangle and make a similar cut from the opposite side.

5 Twist the lemon rind to form a triangle, twisting the ends to secure the shape. Add to the drink with sprigs of fresh lemon balm or mint leaves and serve immediately.

Chilli Vodkatini

Not quite a Martini, but almost. Over the years the proportions of spirit to vermouth have varied widely, with the vodka becoming almost overwhelming. The chillies give this version an extra punch.

Serves 1

INGREDIENTS
1 measure/25 ml/1½ tbsp chilli vodka
   (see Steeped Spirits, page 13)
ice cubes
5 ml/1 tsp medium or dry
   French vermouth
2 small pickled or vodka-soaked chillies and
   1 pitted green olive, to decorate

1 Add the chilli vodka to a tall glass of ice and mix for about 30 seconds, until the outside of the glass has become frosted.

VARIATIONS: For the classic Martini, use gin, but serve with a twist of lemon. Mix plain vodka and dry vermouth for a Vodka Martini. Add a pearl onion and it becomes a Vodka Gibson.

2 Add the vermouth to a chilled cocktail glass and swirl it round the inside of the glass, to moisten it. Discard any remaining vermouth.

3 Cut one of the chillies in half and discard the seeds. Stuff the pitted green olive with the chilli.

4 Thread the stuffed olive on to a cocktail stick, together with the remaining chilli.

5 Strain the cocktail into the prepared cocktail glass. Add the olive and chilli decoration to the drink before serving.

Gibson

Well loved in Japan, this is a version of the Martini with two small white onions in it, rather than the twist of lemon. You may prefer a little more gin.

Serves 1

INGREDIENTS
10 ml/2 tsp extra-dry vermouth
ice cubes
20 ml/4 tsp extra-dry gin
2 pearl onions, to decorate

1 Pour the vermouth into a glass of ice, stir briskly and then pour out. Only the vermouth that clings to the ice and glass should be used.

2 Add the gin and stir for at least 30 seconds, to chill well. Strain into a cocktail glass either on the rocks or straight up.

3 Thread the pearl onions on to a cocktail stick and add to the drink before serving.

VARIATION: Add a touch more dry vermouth and a twist of lemon and you have an Australian Kangaroo.

Perfect Manhattan

It is a matter of preference whether you use sweet or dry vermouth or a mixture. If you are only using one type, add a dash of angostura bitters.

Serves 1

INGREDIENTS
2 measures/45 ml/3 tbsp rye whisky
5 ml/1 tsp sweet Italian vermouth
5 ml/1 tsp dry French vermouth
ice cubes
lemon rind and a maraschino cherry,
    to decorate

1 Pour the rye whisky and sweet and dry vermouths into a tall glass of ice. Stir well for about 30 seconds, to mix and chill. Strain, on the rocks or straight up, into a chilled cocktail glass.

2 Using a cannelle knife (zester), pare away a small, thin strip of lemon rind. Tie it into a knot – this will help release the oils from the rind – and drop it into the cocktail.

3 To finish, add a maraschino cherry with its stalk intact. Serve immediately.

Gall Bracer

Short and smart, this drink is traditionally served with a maraschino cherry for a woman, but without for a man.

Serves 1

INGREDIENTS
ice cubes
2 dashes angostura bitters
2 dashes grenadine
2 measures/45 ml/3 tbsp whisky
lemon rind
maraschino cherry, to decorate (optional)

1 Half-fill a tall glass with ice. Add the angostura bitters, grenadine and whisky and stir well to chill.

2 Place some ice in a shorts tumbler and pour the cocktail over it.

3 Holding the piece of lemon rind between your fingers, squeeze out the oils and juices into the cocktail. Discard the lemon rind. Add a maraschino cherry if you are making the cocktail for a woman. Serve the drink immediately.

Bitter Gimlet

An old-fashioned aperitif, which could easily be turned into a longer drink by topping up with chilled tonic or soda water.

Serves 1

INGREDIENTS
1 lime, cut into wedges
cracked ice and ice cubes
1 measure/25 ml/1½ tbsp gin
2 dashes angostura bitters
slice and rind of lime,
    to decorate

1 Place the lime wedges at the bottom of a tall glass and, using a muddler, press the juice out of the fruit.

2 Add cracked ice, the gin and the angostura bitters and stir well until cold. Strain the cocktail into a shorts tumbler over ice cubes.

3 Add a triangle of lime rind (see Kew Pimm's) and use a slice of lime to decorate the rim of the glass. Serve.

VARIATION: Add a dash or two of crème de menthe to create a Fallen Angel.

Wilga Hill Boomerang

This fresh and fruity sundowner is mixed in a large glass half-full of ice cubes, and is served super-cold.

Serves 1

INGREDIENTS
1 measure/25 ml/1½ tbsp gin
5 ml/1 tsp dry vermouth
5 ml/1 tsp sweet vermouth
1 measure/25 ml/1½ tbsp clear apple juice
ice cubes
1 dash angostura bitters
2 dashes maraschino cherry juice
strip of orange rind and a maraschino cherry,
    to decorate

1 Pour the gin, dry and sweet vermouths and apple juice into a tall glass half-filled with ice, and stir until the outside of the glass has frosted.

2 Pour the angostura bitters and maraschino juice into a highball glass and add ice cubes.

3 Strain the gin and vermouths into a shorts tumbler. Curl the strip of orange rind and add to the cocktail with a maraschino cherry. Serve.

East India

This short and elegant drink can be served as an aperitif, dressed with a twist of lime rind and a maraschino cherry.

Serves 1

INGREDIENTS
15 ml/1 tbsp brandy
2 dashes white curaçao
2 dashes pineapple juice
2 dashes angostura bitters
ice cubes
1 lime and a maraschino cherry,
    to decorate

1 Put the brandy, curaçao, pineapple juice and bitters into a tall glass of ice. Stir the cocktail well for about 20 seconds until chilled, then strain into a shorts tumbler over the ice.

2 Using a cannelle knife, remove a thin piece of rind from the lime, taking care to leave the white pith behind.

3 Tightly twist the rind into a coil, hold for a few seconds, and add to the drink with a maraschino cherry. Serve.

B52

The liqueurs are carefully poured to create the distinctive layers in this cocktail. It has a striking appearance and luxurious taste.

Serves 1

INGREDIENTS
1 measure/25 ml/1½ tbsp Kahlúa
1 measure/25 ml/1½ tbsp Grand Marnier
1 measure/25 ml/1½ tbsp Bailey's
    Irish Cream

1 Pour a 2 cm/¾ in layer of Kahlúa into a *pousse-café* glass.

2 Hold a cold teaspoon upside-down, only just touching the surface of the Kahlúa and the side of the glass.

VARIATION: Create a similar layered effect with equal quantities of Kahlúa, vodka and Bailey's.

3 Slowly and carefully pour the Grand Marnier over the back of the teaspoon, to create a second layer.

4 In the same way, carefully pour the Bailey's Irish Cream over the back of a second clean teaspoon, to create a final layer. This layer will in fact form the middle layer, pushing the Grand Marnier to the top. Serve.

Hooded Claw

Syrupy-sweet prune juice with Amaretto and Cointreau makes a delicious digestif when poured over crushed ice.

Serves 1

INGREDIENTS
30 ml/2 tbsp prune juice
10 ml/2 tsp Amaretto
5 ml/1 tsp Cointreau
crushed ice and ice cubes

1 Pour the prune juice, Amaretto and Cointreau together into a cocktail shaker half-filled with ice.

2 Shake the cocktail for 20 seconds, to ensure that it is thoroughly mixed and chilled.

3 Loosely fill a small liqueur glass with crushed ice until it reaches almost to the rim. Strain the prepared cocktail into the liquer glass, add a short drinking straw, if you like, and serve the cocktail immediately.

Morning Glory Fizz

A good brunch drink, which should be consumed as soon as it is made, before it loses its flavour and bubbles.

Serves 1

INGREDIENTS
15 ml/1 tbsp brandy
5 ml/1 tsp orange curaçao
5 ml/1 tsp lemon juice
1 dash anisette
ice cubes
2 dashes angostura bitters
soda water, chilled, to taste
thin strip of lemon rind, to decorate

1 Pour the brandy, orange curaçao, lemon juice and anisette into a cocktail shaker containing ice and shake for 20 seconds.

2 Strain the drink into a small, chilled highball glass. Add the angostura bitters to taste and top up with soda water.

3 Curl the thin strip of lemon rind into a tight coil and add to the cocktail before serving.

Mai Tai

Pineapple and orange juices make this a very refreshing party drink that slips down easily, but beware – it is strong.

Serves 1

INGREDIENTS
1 measure/25 ml/1½ tbsp white rum
1 measure/25 ml/1½ tbsp dark rum
1 measure/25 ml/1½ tbsp apricot
　brandy
cracked and crushed ice
3 measures/70 ml/4½ tbsp orange juice,
　chilled
3 measures/70 ml/4½ tbsp pineapple
　juice, chilled
1 measure/25 ml/1½ tbsp grenadine

1 Add the white and dark rum and apricot brandy to a cocktail shaker half-full of cracked ice. Add the well chilled orange and pineapple juices.

2 Shake together well for about 20 seconds or until the outside of the cocktail shaker feels cold. Strain into a highball glass of crushed ice.

3 Slowly pour the grenadine into the glass so that it falls to the bottom of the drink to make a glowing red layer. Serve immediately.

Moscow Mule

This uses a large quantity of angostura bitters for its flavour and colour and enough vodka to give a real kick.

Serves 1

INGREDIENTS
2 measures/45 ml/3 tbsp vodka
6 dashes angostura bitters
dash of lime cordial
10 ml/2 tsp lime juice
ice cubes
3 measures/70 ml/4½ tbsp ginger beer
slices of lime, to decorate

1 Pour the vodka, angostura bitters, lime cordial and fresh lime juice into a bar glass of ice. Mix together well to blend.

2 Strain into a highball glass containing a couple of ice cubes. Top up the mixture with ginger beer.

3 Cut a few slices of lime in half and add them to the drink before serving.

Grasshopper

A minted, creamy cocktail in an attractive shade of green. You can use dark crème de cacao, but the cocktail will not be as colourful.

Serves 1

INGREDIENTS

2 measures/45 ml/3 tbsp crème de menthe
2 measures/45 ml/3 tbsp crème de cacao
2 measures/45 ml/3 tbsp double (heavy) cream
cracked ice
50g/2oz milk chocolate, melted

1 To make the decoration, spread the melted chocolate evenly over a plastic board and leave to cool and harden.

2 Draw the blade of a sharp knife across the hardened chocolate to create curls. Set aside while you prepare the cocktail.

3 Measure the crème de menthe and crème de cacao into a cocktail shaker and add the cream.

4 Add some cracked ice and shake well for 20 seconds. Strain the cocktail into a highball glass of finely cracked ice. Add the chocolate curls to the top of the cocktail and serve.

Long Island Iced Tea

This is a long, potent drink that has an intoxicating effect, although it is well disguised by the ice-cold cola.

Serves 1

INGREDIENTS
cracked ice and ice cubes
10 ml/2 tsp white rum
10 ml/2 tsp vodka
10 ml/2 tsp gin
10 ml/2 tsp Grand Marnier
 or Cointreau
1 measure/25 ml/1½ tbsp cold
 Earl Grey tea
juice of ½ lemon, to taste
cola, chilled, to taste
slices of lemon and a large sprig of
 fresh mint, to decorate

2 Add the cold Earl Grey tea to the spirits in the bar glass. Stir well for 30 seconds, or until thoroughly chilled.

3 Add the lemon juice, to taste. Strain into a highball glass filled with ice cubes and lemon slices.

1 Fill a bar glass with cracked ice and add the rum, vodka, gin and Grand Marnier or Cointreau.

4 Pour in chilled cola, according to taste, and add a sprig of fresh mint to use as a swizzle stick. Serve.

VARIATION: For a simpler version of this drink, use equal quantities of white rum, Cointreau, tequila and lemon juice and top up with cola. Serve over ice and decorate.

COOK'S TIP: Bergamot gives Earl Grey tea its distinctive flavour. Do not be tempted to use any other tea as the flavour will not be the same.

Planter's Punch

This refreshing, old colonial drink originates from the sugar plantations of the West Indies. Fresh fruit decoration adds an exotic touch.

Serves 1

INGREDIENTS
1 measure/25 ml/1½ tbsp
   lime juice
1 measure/25 ml/1½ tbsp
   orange juice (optional)
ice cubes
2 measures/45 ml/3 tbsp dark rum
10 ml/2 tsp grenadine
dash of angostura bitters
soda water or lemonade, chilled
2 peach slices and a physalis,
   to decorate

2 Add a dash of angostura bitters to the bottom of a chilled highball glass filled with ice cubes.

3 Strain the rum and grenadine mixture into the highball glass.

1 Add the lime juice and orange juice, if using, to a bar glass filled with ice. Add the dark rum and grenadine and mix together for about 20 seconds.

4 Top up the cocktail with plenty of well-chilled soda water or lemonade.

5 To decorate the cocktail, make a short cut in two slices of fresh peach and the physalis. Push the fruit on to the edge of the tumbler. Serve the cocktail immediately.

VARIATIONS: Add 1 measure/ 25 ml/1½ tbsp cold Assam tea, prepared to a strength of your own liking, for a different tang. Use other fruit such as strawberries, to decorate.

Blue Hawaiian

This eye-catching drink can be decorated as flamboyantly as Carmen Miranda's headdress with a mixture of fruits and leaves.

Serves 1

INGREDIENTS
1 measure/25 ml/1½ tbsp blue curaçao
1 measure/25 ml/1½ tbsp coconut cream
2 measures/45 ml/3 tbsp white rum
ice cubes
2 measures/45 ml/3 tbsp pineapple juice

TO DECORATE
maraschino cherry
leaves and wedge of pineapple
slice of prickly pear
wedge of lime

3 Add all of the pineapple juice to the blender and process the mixture once more, until it is well blended and frothy.

1 Put the blue curaçao, coconut cream and white rum into a blender. Process very briefly until just mixed and the colour is even.

2 Place the ice cubes between a dishtowel and crush to a fine snow with a wooden mallet or rolling pin.

4 Spoon some crushed ice snow into a large cocktail glass or goblet. Pour the cocktail from the blender over the crushed ice.

VARIATIONS: Pour equal quantities of vodka and blue curaçao over ice. Top up with lemonade for a Blue Lagoon or add equal quantities of gin and curaçao, plus angostura bitters, for a Blue Cloak.

5 Thread the maraschino cherry on to a cocktail stick between the pineapple leaves. Trim the stick close to the leaves. Push another stick through the cherry to secure it to the pineapple wedge. Make a short cut into the prickly pear and lime, then push on to the side of the glass. Serve with drinking straws.

Vodka & Kumquat Lemonade

A mild-sounding name for a strong concoction of kumquat and peppercorn-flavoured vodka and white curaçao. Prepare the vodka-soaked kumquats in advance.

Serves 1

INGREDIENTS
40 g/1½ oz kumquats
60 ml/4 tbsp vodka
3 black peppercorns, cracked (optional)
cracked ice and ice cubes
7.5 ml/1½ tbsp white curaçao or
   orange syrup
7.5 ml/1½ tbsp lemon juice
1 measure/25 ml/1½ tbsp mineral
   or soda water
sprigs of fresh mint, to decorate

2 Fill a jug with cracked ice and then add the curaçao or orange syrup, the lemon juice and the kumquat-flavoured vodka with the sliced kumquats. Using a long swizzle stick, mix together well.

1 Thickly slice the kumquats and add to the vodka in an airtight jar with the cracked black peppercorns, if using. Cover tightly and leave for a couple of hours, overnight or up to a month.

VARIATION: Use home- or ready-made elderflower cordial with gin or vodka, and top up with soda or tonic water.

3 Add the mineral or soda water and a few sprigs of fresh mint and gently stir everything together.

4 Pour the cocktail into a chilled cocktail goblet of ice cubes, and decorate with more mint sprigs. Serve.

Coffee & Chocolate Flip

Since the egg is not cooked, use only the freshest eggs. Drambuie can be used instead of brandy for a hint of honey, but do not then add the sugar. Substitute Tia Maria for the Kahlúa, to make a less sweet version.

Serves 1

INGREDIENTS
1 measure/25 ml/1½ tbsp brandy
1 measure/25 ml/1½ tbsp Kahlúa
5 ml/1 tsp instant coffee granules
3 measures/70 ml/4½ tbsp double (heavy) cream
1 egg
5 ml/1 tsp caster (superfine) sugar
crushed ice
drinking chocolate powder or grated chocolate, to decorate

1 In a small saucepan, gently warm together the brandy, Kahlúa, instant coffee granules and double cream. Allow to cool.

VARIATION: Shake together equal quantities of Kahlúa, chocolate-flavoured milk and coffee. Serve over ice cubes.

2 Separate the egg and lightly beat the egg white, with a fork or whisk, until frothy and white. In a separate bowl or bar glass, beat the egg yolk with the sugar.

3 Whisk the cream mixture into the beaten egg yolk and sugar. Add the egg white and pour the mixture briefly back and forth between two bar glasses, until the mixture is smooth.

4 Pour into a tall cocktail goblet over coarsely crushed ice and sprinkle the top with drinking chocolate powder or grated chocolate before serving.

Citrus Refresher

What could be more cooling and invigorating on a hot summer's day?

Serves 1

INGREDIENTS
3 limes
1 orange
½ grapefruit
150 ml/¼ pint/⅔ cup water
20 g/¾ oz caster (superfine) sugar
ice cubes, to serve
extra fruit wedges, to decorate

1 Squeeze the juice from the limes, orange and grapefruit. Some fruit pulp may collect along with the juice. This should also be used, once any seeds have been discarded.

2 Pour the citrus juices into a large jug. Add the water and sugar and stir until all the sugar has dissolved.

3 Chill for 1 hour before serving with ice and fruit wedges. Store, covered, for 2–3 days in the fridge.

Melon Cooler

This refreshing drink is attractively coloured with the hue of the watermelon.

Serves 1

INGREDIENTS
¼ small watermelon
250 ml/8 fl oz/1 cup chilled water
juice of ½ lime
honey, to taste
ice cubes, to serve

1 Remove the skin from the watermelon, and scrape out and discard the black seeds. Cut the watermelon flesh into large chunks.

2 Place the melon chunks in a large bowl, pour over the chilled water and leave to stand for 10 minutes.

3 Tip the mixture into a large sieve set over a bowl. Using a wooden spoon, press gently on the fruit to extract all the liquid.

4 Stir in the lime juice and sweeten to taste with honey. Pour into a highball glass, add ice cubes and stir. Serve.

Horse's Fall

A long, cool drink to serve in warm weather. The addition of strongly flavoured tea is a matter of taste and preference.

Serves 1

INGREDIENTS
1 lemon
1 dash angostura bitters
2 measures/45 ml/3 tbsp raspberry, Orange Pekoe or Assam tea, chilled (optional)
1 measure/25 ml/1½ tbsp clear, unsweetened apple juice
ice cubes
5 measures/120 ml/4 fl oz/½ cup dry ginger ale or lemonade, chilled

1 Cut the peel from the lemon in one thin, continuous strip and use to line and decorate a long cocktail glass. Chill the glass until required.

2 Add a dash of angostura bitters to the bottom of the glass.

3 Measure the tea, if using, into a cocktail shaker and add the apple juice and ice cubes. Shake everything together for about 20 seconds.

4 Strain the apple juice mixture into the prepared, chilled cocktail goblet. Top up with chilled ginger ale or lemonade, to taste. Serve at once.

VARIATION: For an alcoholic version, substitute Calvados or brandy for the flavoured tea to create a Horse's Neck.

COOK'S TIP: You can use apple juice from a carton for this cocktail, or try apple concentrate mixed with water which is more economical and lasts longer in the fridge. It is available from health food stores.

Scarlet Lady

This drink could easily pass as an alcoholic wine-based cocktail.

Serves 1

INGREDIENTS
115 g/4 oz honeydew melon or watermelon
5 small red grapes
3 measures/70 ml/4½ tbsp unsweetened
    red grape juice
ice cubes

TO DECORATE
red grapes
1 egg white, lightly beaten
15 g/½ oz caster (superfine) sugar

1 Seed the melon. Cut the melon and
grapes in a blender and process until
they form a smooth purée.

2 Add the red grape juice and
continue to process for another
minute. Strain into a bar glass of ice
and stir until chilled.

3 To make the decoration, dip the
grapes in beaten egg white and roll in
caster sugar. Leave to dry.

4 Pour the fruit juice mixture into a
chilled cocktail glass and decorate with
sugar-frosted grapes threaded on to a
cocktail stick.

VARIATION: Top up the purée
with red grape juice and tonic.

Steel Works

A thirst-quenching drink, which is ideal to serve at any time.

Serves 1

INGREDIENTS

2 measures/45 ml/3 tbsp passion-fruit cordial
1 dash angostura bitters
ice cubes
3 measures/70 ml/4½ tbsp soda water, chilled
3 measures/70 ml/4½ tbsp lemonade, chilled
1 passion fruit

1 Pour the cordial straight into a Collins glass. Add the angostura bitters and then some ice cubes.

VARIATION: For a Rock Shandy, pour equal quantities of lemonade and soda on to bitters.

2 Top up the drink with the chilled soda water and lemonade and stir briefly to mix together.

3 Cut the passion fruit in half, if using, scoop the seeds and flesh from the fruit and add to the drink. Stir the cocktail gently before serving. Add drinking straws, if you like.

Fruit & Ginger Ale

Roasting the fruit with cloves gives this drink its wonderful, unique flavour.

Serves 4–6

INGREDIENTS
1 medium cooking apple
1 orange, scrubbed
1 lemon, scrubbed
20 whole cloves
7.5 cm/3 in fresh root ginger, peeled
25 g/1 oz/soft brown sugar
300 ml/½ pint/1¼ cups boiling water
cracked ice
about 350 ml/12 fl oz/1½ cups
   bitter lemon or
   non-alcoholic wine
wedges of orange rind and
   whole cloves, to decorate

2 Quarter the orange and lemon and pulp the apple, discarding the skin and core. Finely grate the ginger. Place the fruit and ginger together in a bowl with the soft brown sugar.

3 Add 300 ml/½ pint/1¼ cups boiling water. Using a spoon, squeeze the fruit to release more flavour. Cover and leave to cool for an hour or overnight, if possible.

1 Preheat the oven to 200°C/400°F/ Gas 6. Score the apple around the middle and stud the orange and lemon with the whole cloves. Bake them in the oven for 25 minutes until soft and completely cooked through.

COOK'S TIP: Start preparations the day before, if possible.

4 Strain into a jug of cracked ice and use a spoon to press out all the juices from the fruit. Add the bitter lemon or non-alcoholic wine, to taste. Serve in a long glass, decorated with orange rind studded with cloves.

Blushing Piña Colada

A deliciously creamy cocktail that tastes as good as it looks. Do not be tempted to put roughly crushed ice into the blender; it will not be as smooth and will ruin the blades. Make sure you crush it well first.

Serves 1

INGREDIENTS
½ banana, peeled and sliced
½ thick slice pineapple, peeled
30 ml/2 tbsp pineapple juice
1 scoop strawberry ice cream
   or strawberry sorbet
10 ml/2 tsp coconut milk
finely crushed ice
15 ml/1 tbsp grenadine
maraschino cherry, to decorate

1 Roughly chop the banana. Cut a small wedge from the pineapple for decoration, and reserve. Cut up the remainder of the pineapple and add to the blender with the banana.

VARIATION: For a Passionate Encounter, blend 2 scoops passion-fruit sorbet and 15 ml/1 tbsp coconut milk with a measure each of pineapple and apricot juice.

2 Add the pineapple juice to the blender and process until the mixture is a smooth purée.

3 Add the strawberry ice cream or sorbet with the coconut milk and a small scoop of finely crushed ice. Process until smooth.

4 Pour into a well-chilled large cocktail goblet. Pour the grenadine syrup slowly on top of the Piña Colada; it will filter through the drink in a dappled effect.

5 For the decoration, make a short cut into the maraschino cherry and reserved pineapple wedge and push the fruit on to the edge of the glass. Serve the cocktail immediately with drinking straws.

Index

This edition is published by Lorenz Books,
an imprint of Anness Publishing Ltd,
108 Great Russell Street, London WC1B 3NA info@anness.com
www.lorenzbooks.com; www.annesspublishing.com

© Anness Publishing Limited 2015

If you like the images in this book and would like to investigate
using them for publishing, promotions or advertising, please visit
our website www.practicalpictures.com for more information.

Publisher: Joanna Lorenz
Editor: Valerie Ferguson & Helen Sudell
Designer: Andrew Heath
Production Controller: Steve Lang

Recipes contributed by: Oona van den Berg, Bridget Jones,
Jane Milton, Stuart Walton, Pamela Westland.

Photography: Steve Baxter, James Duncan, Nelson Hargreaves,
Janine Hosegood, Simon Smith.

A CIP catalogue record for this book is available from the
British Library

COOK'S NOTES

Bracketed terms are intended for American readers.

For all recipes, quantities are given in both metric and imperial
measures and, where appropriate, in standard cups and spoons.
Follow one set of measures, but not a mixture, because they are
not interchangeable.

Standard spoon and cup measures are level. 1 tsp = 5ml, 1 tbsp =
15ml, 1 cup = 250ml/8fl oz. Australian standard tablespoons are
20ml. Australian readers should use 3 tsp
in place of 1 tbsp for measuring small quantities.

American pints are 16fl oz/2 cups. American readers should use
20fl oz/2.5 cups in place of 1 pint when measuring liquids.

Electric oven temperatures in this book are for conventional
ovens. When using a fan oven, the temperature will probably
need to be reduced by about 10–20°C/20–40°F. Since ovens
vary, you should check with your instruction's instruction
book for guidance.

Medium (US large) eggs are used unless otherwise stated.

PUBLISHER'S NOTE:

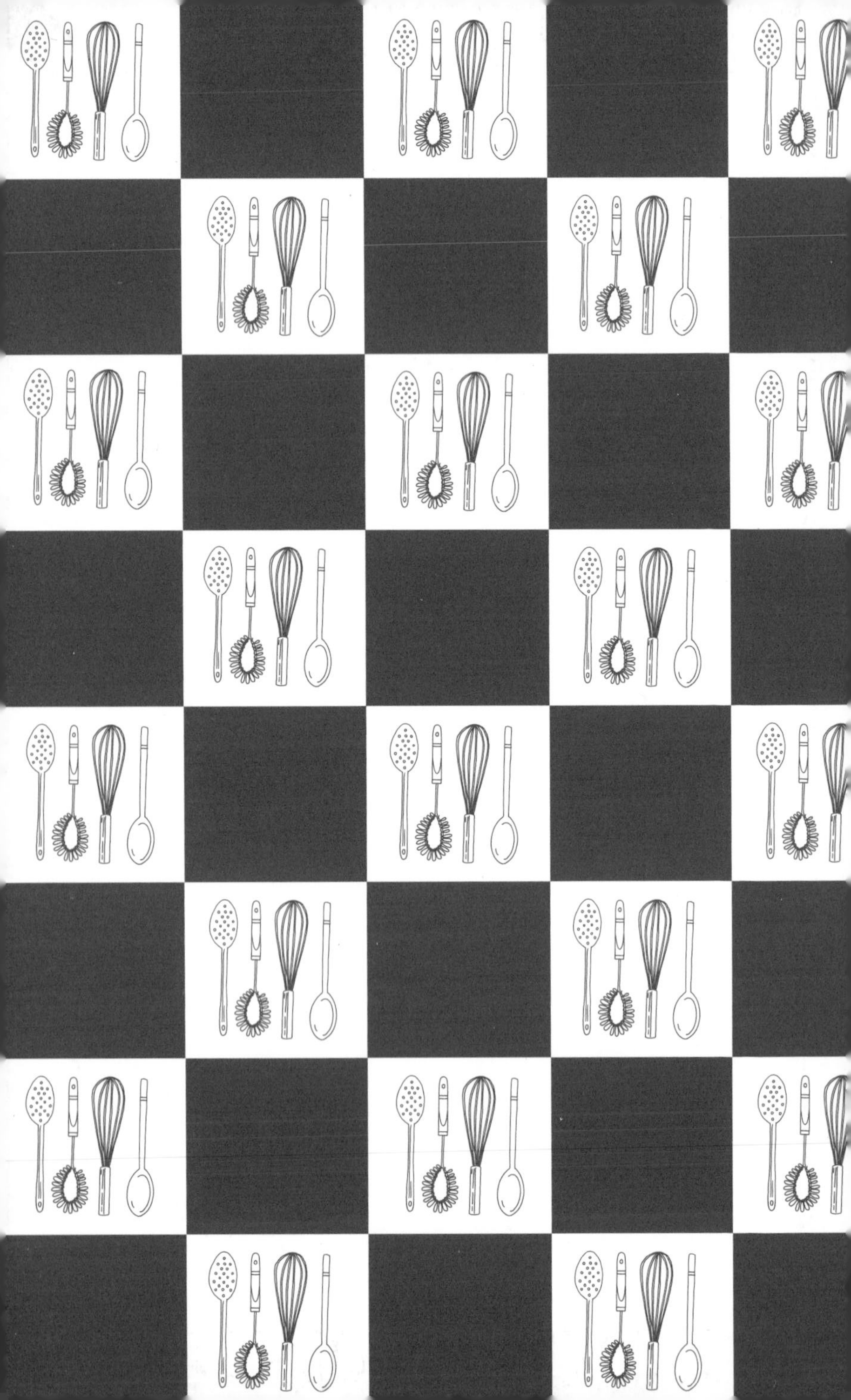